THE ARCHAEOLOGICAL EXPLORATIONS OF ASSAM

A BRIEF HISTORY OF EXPLORATIONS IN ASSAM

ISHWAR SINGH

I am dedicating this book to my parents Sardar Pal Singh and Sardarni Amarjit Kaur who brought me into this beautiful world and made me capable of being what I am today.

Contents

Foreword

Ishwar Singh have more than ten years of experience in writing and in research activities. He is a tremendous writer. He is doing excellent job by writing about archaeological explorations of Assam. He had shown very keen interest in the field of archaeological resources and other cultural issues.

He is also a very excellent teacher and also having deep knowledge about the social science issues. I have always seen him working very hard for his various books. He just want to express about the Indian culture to our new generations in a simple and brief manner. I wish him all the very best for his new book.

Birinder Pal Kaur

Preface

Dear Readers

It gives me great pleasure to present before you the collection of my notes in the form of a book. In this book, I have tried to use very simple language, quality photographs regarding situation of our archeological excavations.

As you read the title of this book which is 'The Archaeological Explorations of Assam' you can understand the motive of this book. This book talks about the present situation of our archeological Sites.

I have tried to do research on our precious archeological sites so that we can understand the medieval period and being engaged with our traditional culture.

I just want to explore the some important archeological sites of Assam so that our future generations could know about importance of it. I have tried to express my views in very short words and just briefly explain the various sites.

I think you will enjoy this book and engage yourself in a thorough reading.

Thank You

Acknowledgements

Writing a book is harder than I thought and more rewarding than I could have ever imagined. None of this would have been possible without my best friend, Malkeet Singh Sohal. He was the first friend I made when I moved to Tawi Engineering College, Pathankot. He stood by me during every struggle and all my successes. That is true friendship.

I'm eternally grateful to my father Pal Singh, who took in an extra mouth to feed when he didn't have to. He taught me discipline, tough love, manners, respect, and so much more that has helped me succeed in life. I truly have no idea where I'd be if he hadn't given me a roof over my head whom I desperately needed at that age.

To my father-in-law Narinder Singh for their moral support during the up and downs in my life. He taught me how to live positive even in the worst situations by his sharing his personal experiances. He is the man who suggest me to write a book in your life because it will be your book by which you will be remembered in future.

To Dr. Davinder Singh, who took a chance on a twenty-nine-year-old kid and let him run his offices in Akal Academy, Baru Sahib, Himachal Pradesh. He never saw my age, my race, or my lack of formal education. He just saw a kid hungry to learn, hungry to grow, and hungry to succeed in teaching. He never stopped me; he only encouraged me.

Writing a book about the archaeological explorations is a surreal process. I'm forever indebted to Birinder Pal Kaur and Naginder Pal Singh for their editorial help, keen insight, and ongoing support in bringing my research to life. It is because of their efforts and encouragement that I have a legacy to pass on to my family where one didn't exist before.

To everyone at the Scribe Tribe who enables me to be the teacher of a organisation that I'm honored to be a part of, thank you for letting me serve, for being a part of our amazing organisation, and for showing up every day and helping more authors turn their ideas into books.

To my family. To Mom Amarjit Kaur: for always being the person I could turn to during those dark and desperate years. She sustained me in ways that I never knew that I needed. To my little brother, Hardeep Singh: thank you for letting me know that you had nothing but great memories of me. So thankful to have you back in my life.

Finally, to all those who have been a part of my getting there: Sukhbir Singh, Devinder Kumar Sharma, Sumeet Kaur, Rinkpal Singh, Yadwinder Singh, Iqbal Singh, Kulwinder Kaur, Surinder Singh, Amandeep Singh.

I want to thank EVERYONE who ever said anything positive to me or taught me something. I heard it all, and it meant something.

I want to thank God most of all, because without God I wouldn't be able to do any of this.

Prologue

An archaeological site is a site which tells us about the history of our ansectors. It is an archaeological site which tells us about the living standards, economic activities, food habbits, religious practices, kingdoms, rulers, ornaments and fashion of adopted by our forefathers.

The Archaeological explorations in Assam are also very important sources of information. The explorations in Assam majorly puts light on evidences related to the religions and the kingdoms of medieval period. In this book, I have discussed about the brief history of such religious and other archaeological sites.

CHAPTER ONE

Introduction

"New Excavated Archaeological Sites always tells us to rethink about the history"

Ishwar Singh

India is a country of various cultural diversity and it is our duty to preserve and protect this diversity. In this book, I will talk about Assam. Assam is located at north eastern front of India. Assam is very rich in culture and have very

important archaeological sites.

The important archaeological sites in assam includes Ambari, Madan Kamdev, Sri Surya Pahar, Bamuni Hills, Ahom Raja's Palace, Deopahar, Moterjhar Temple, Raush Movement and Chatrakar temple.

These archaeological sites have excellent stone carvations, design on the stones, symmetrical shapes.

CHAPTER TWO

Ambari

Among the various important archaeological sites in Assam, Ambari has its great importance. This archaeological site is representing old civilisation of Assam.

The Ambari Archaeological Site, situated in the heart of the Guwahati city in Kamrup District of Assam was accidentally discovered in course of digging the foundation for the building of the Reserve Bank of India in 1969. From 1970 to 2003 the site was excavated by different

excavators.

The most important discovery of the excavation of Ambari Archaeological Site during the field season 2008-09 is flight of steps made of bricks leading to the tank.

Besides, the excavation has revealed two floors and two hearths resting on the natural soil significantly.

The ceramic industry of the site is dominated by Kaolin ware, Red ware, Buff ware and few Grey wares, which are available in medium and coarse fabrics and occasionally applied with slip. All the pot sherds found are of wheel-turned, although a small percentage of handmade potteries is also recovered.[1]

Ruins of Ambari [Source: www.asiguwahaticircle.gov.in]

Refrences

....

1. www.asiguwahaticircle.gov.in

CHAPTER THREE

Madan Kamdev

Have you ever heared about Khujraho temples? These are very famous temples in india which are located in present day Madhya Pradesh. Khujraho Temples are popular for their unique architecture styles and graceful sculptures. But here we are going to talk about Assam. In Assam we have some sculptures similar to Khujraho.

Madan Kamdev is an archaeological site in Baihata Chariali, Kamrup, Assam. The place dates back to the 9th and 10th century A.D. The excavation and ruins is dated back to the Pala dynasty of Kamarupa.[1]

This Temple complex is also known as 'Khujraho of Assam'.[2]

It is believed that Kama or Madan, the God of Love was reborn in this place after being turn into ashes by angry Lord Shiva. One school believes that Madan was reborn and united to his wife Rati in this tiny hillock. Another school argue that the name Madan Kamdev has romantic association with the place, because of the numerous erotic sculptures.[3]

Ruins of Madan Kamdev Temple [Source: www.abhijna-emuseum.com]

Ruins of Madan Kamdev Temple [Source: www.travellingslacker.com]

Refrences

1. www.indiatravelnext.com.
2. www.livehistoryindia.com
3. www.kamrup.assam.gov.in

CHAPTER FOUR

Sri Surya Pahar

Sri Surya Pahar Archaeological site is especially famous for the huge number of Shivlingas spreaded around the mountain. It is also a unique experience, when you will observe such numbers of monuments around you.

Sri Surya Pahar is a hilly terrain where several rock-cut Shivalingas, votive stupas and the deities of Hindu, Buddhist and Jain pantheon are scattered in an area of about one kilometer. The site is centered on the hills (Pahar) of Sri

Surya which is profusely filled up with Shiva Lingas (Lingam).[1]

Hinduism was practiced in Ancient Assam even before the 4th century CE during the time when it finds a textual mention. The early dynasties of the area were Buddhist religion namely the Varmanas dynasty (350-650 CE), the Palas of Bengal (9000-1100 CE) and the Mlechchha dynasty (655-900 CE). These dynasties ruled from Assam capital Pragjyotishpura for more than 800 years until the 13th century of medieval Ahoms.

Numerous scholars came with the opinion that this site which mainly flourished during the pe-Ahom era was the hub of trade as the place is located near the bank of the River Brahmaputra. At this place travelers and people related to trade connected with each other which resulted in forming a network of different cultures and religious beliefs.[2]

Ruins of Sri Surya Pahar [Source: www.sentinelassam.com]

Refrences

....

1. "Surya temple,Surya pahar temple,Surya pahar,Assam". www.religiousportal.com. 1 January 1980. Retrieved 29 March 2013.

2. www.sentinelassam.com

CHAPTER FIVE

Bamuni Hills

The Sculptures found in the Bamuni hills also has its unique importance in the history of Assam's archaeology. These Sculptures very unique features such as their artistic structure. The sculptures of different deities are present here. This important site needs more protection for their long term survival.

The ruins of Bamuni Hills are famous for their exemplary artistic finesse. The sculptural remains date back to the ninth and tenth century A.D.[1]

According to the Archaeological Survey of India (ASI), the style of the excavations hints that they were raised during the Gupta period. The stone carvings on the walls of the Bamuni Hills also make for an interesting sight and attract visitors with their artistic beauty. A popular belief hints that the ruins might have belonged to a temple dedicated to Lord Vishnu.[2]

Ruins of Bamuni Hills [Source: www.sonitpur.gov.in]

Refrences

....

1. Source: www.sonitpur.gov.in
2. www.incredibleindia.org

CHAPTER SIX

Ahom Raja's Palace

Whenever we read the history of our rebellions against the cruel kingdoms, you will find the name of Ahoms. Ahom Kings were very passionate for their territories and had no fear of anyone and fought many wars against their enemies so bravely.

Ahom is a tribal group belong to our present state of Assam. Ahoms were great warriors and they had fought wars against Mughals and defeated them 17 times.

Ahom Raja's palace is an historic building in Garhgaon, Assam State, India. Garhgaon was the home of the Alom dynasty. The palace was built by king Rajeswar Singha in 1752 CE.[1]

Ahom Raja's Palace [Source: www.trekearth.com]

Refrences

....

1. "Archaeological Survey of India(ASI), Guwahati Circle, Assam". asiguwahaticircle.gov.in. Retrieved 2021-02-10.

CHAPTER SEVEN

Deopahar

The artistic impression of stone carvations of various statues in Deopahar stone temple is very impressive. The Deopahar stone temple site is one of the richest site in explorations. Various types of architectural ruins were obtained from this site. It is also become a most attractive tourist site now a days.

The ancient stone temple and sculptures uncovered at this site are fine specimens of ancient art that represent the interconnection between Aryan (Brahmanical) art and local art, thus, providing enough data for the historians to determine the period of time it was created.[1]

The intricate architectural style of the Deopahar stone temple is indicative of the fact that it belongs to the period somewhere between 10th and 11th century AD.[2]

An English tea planter named Thomas Guardthei was the first to highlight the significance and complexity of the unique sculpture and architecture of the broken Shiva temple at Deopahar. The stone temple was erected on a monolithic floor. The temple has a big ceiling slab engraved with a large lotus bearing a relief of Vidyadhara holding a scarf and a necklace by both hands. The vast range of sculptured stone blocks were carved out of Precambrian rocks. The stone blocks in the base of the temple were stabilized together with iron hinges which can be clearly seen.[3]

Ruins of Deopahar Stone Temple [Source: www.mapsus.net]

Ruins of Deopahar Stone Temple [Source: www.mapsus.net]

Ruins of Deopahar Stone Temple [Source: www.mapsus.net]

Refrences

....

1. Sarmah, Dr. Bijoy (September 1, 2020). "A Historical Study of the Archaeological Remains of Deopahar, Numaligarh" (PDF). SAMPRITI. VI (II): 667–679 – via researchgate.net.

2. "Home | Directorate of Archaeology | Government Of Assam, India". archaeology.assam.gov.in.

3. "Temple ruins on Dhansiri bank". www.telegraphindia.com.

CHAPTER EIGHT

Moterjhar Temple

The Moterjhar Temple is made up of bricks, roof extended by steel sheds. This site is surrounded by a large ground having green grass. Around the ground there are number of trees planted.

A brick-built temple of the Koch period is to be found here. This site has a tank. Evidence of a brick structure of a secular nature is also found buried in the site, which is yet to be explored fully.[1]

Ruins of Moterjhar Temple [Source: www.archaeology.assam.gov.in]

Refrences

1. www.archaeology.assam.gov.in

CHAPTER NINE

Raush Monument

The Raush monument is just a small monument and now protected as the grave of an European.

The Raush Monument is the grave of an European salt trader located at Bandar Kanda hillock near the Court of the Chief Judicial Magistrate in Goalpara. The hillock has a unique location surrounded as it is by the River Brahmaputra on three directions. It housed a colony of British and other European officials. The existence of several graves and evidence of

British buildings point towards that. The graves commemoratethe glory of the British officials who had controlled administration from this locality in Goalpara.[1]

Ruins of Raush Monument [Source: www.archaeology.assam.gov.in]

Refrences

1. www.archaeology.assam.gov.in

CHAPTER TEN

Chatrakar Temple

The Chatrakar Temple also has its own importance in the history of archaeology. The architectural qualities of the Chatrakar Temple is a site of attraction. The Stone carvations of famous deities is still representing the dedication of the artists of that period.

The site located on devottar land has a group of three temples dedicated to Siva, Visnu and Mangalchandi of the late mediaeval period. Built during the reign of the Ahom king

Kamaleswar Singha, (1795-1810), the Chatrakar temple is an important saktashrine.

A few stone sculptures of the stone temple that existed on this site during the early mediaeval period are found here. A few sculptures of the early mediaeval phase have been embedded in the outer walls of the temples. A beautifully carved stone image of Vamshigopalais enshrined in the Visnu temple here.[1]

Stone image of Vamshigopalais [Source: www.archaeology.assam.gov.in]

Refrences

....

1. www.archaeology.assam.gov.in

CHAPTER ELEVEN

Umachal Rock Inscription

Rock inscriptions are the very useful source of information through which our historians got lots of factful information about ancient as well as medieval period. These were the rock inscriptions from where got the useful information of Mauryan Empire and Gupta Empire.

There are some rock inscriptions, on which historians are still doing research to decipher it and want to know messages conveyed by ancient and medieval civilisations during their period.

Umachal Rock Inscription is located on Umachal in Nilachal hill facing the River Brahmaputra. This rock-cut inscription is engraved in *brahmi* language.

The information obtained from 'Umachal Rock Inscription' is "This cave (temple) of the illustrious Lord Balabhadra has been constructed by maharajadhiraja Sri Surendra Varmana".[1]

Umachal Rock Inscription [Source: www.archaeology.assam.gov.in]

Refrences

1. www.archaeology.assam.gov.in

CHAPTER TWELVE

Nazirakhat Archaeological Site

The Nazirakhat Archaeological Site is a environmentally rich site. You will observe the healthy experience of the nature around this site.

The Nazirakhat Archaeological Site is known historically as Ganesh mandir, as this site possibly had a stone temple dedicated to Lord Ganesa. This site has ruins of a stone temple

belonging to the late mediaeval period.

The temple was erected on the bank of the Karchiya river and numerous stone fragments and temple components are to be found on this site, including two rock cut sculptures of Ganesa. The geographical location of the Nazirakhat Archaeological Site is one diversified by hills and plains and altogether generates an environment of natural charm enriched with cultural heritage.[1]

Nazirakhat Archaeological Site [Source: www.archaeology.assam.gov.in]

Refrences

1. www.archaeology.assam.gov.in

Conclusion

We had started our journey from Ambari archaeological site. As we know this site was accidentally discovered. It needs more care by the government due to people's activity around this site.

The situation of Madan Kamdev Temple is also not good. Just the major ruins of the temple left. Major carved stones had been damaged.

In the case of Bamuni Hills, the excavations available there are the examples of fine art. The small statues designed on the stone bed are so beautiful.

Rest of the sites are in good conditions. we can't

say that there is no need of protection, there is the need of protection and proper care of these sites. Whether the government of assam is already showing his efforts but to secure our cultural heritage and protect it for the future generations, is not the duty of government only, it is the duty of all citizens of our country also.

Whenever you are planning to visit such archaeological sites, just remember one thing, you will not just only visit the site, there you will also observe the talents of our ancestors that is how skilled they were? Always give respect to such archaeological sites and try to learn something new from such sites.

Never ever use any pen or sketch on such precious monuments. If we are damaging such scriptures, it is reflecting that how foolish we are. That's the message from my side and this is also a purpose of my life to publish such books for our new generations so that they could aware of importance of such sites.

Printed by Libri Plureos GmbH in Hamburg, Germany